T0147154

THE KINGDOM OF GOD

DONT MISS THE MESSAGE JESUS
WANTS YOU TO KNOW

Rhonda Varnado

WESTBOW
PRESS®
A DIVISION OF THOMAS NELSON
& ZONDERVAN

Copyright © 2022 Rhonda Varnado.

All rights reserved. No part of this book may be used or reproduced by any means, graphic, electronic, or mechanical, including photocopying, recording, taping or by any information storage retrieval system without the written permission of the author except in the case of brief quotations embodied in critical articles and reviews.

This book is a work of non-fiction. Unless otherwise noted, the author and the publisher make no explicit guarantees as to the accuracy of the information contained in this book and in some cases, names of people and places have been altered to protect their privacy.

WestBow Press books may be ordered through booksellers or by contacting:

WestBow Press
A Division of Thomas Nelson & Zondervan
1663 Liberty Drive
Bloomington, IN 47403
www.westbowpress.com
844-714-3454

Because of the dynamic nature of the Internet, any web addresses or links contained in this book may have changed since publication and may no longer be valid. The views expressed in this work are solely those of the author and do not necessarily reflect the views of the publisher, and the publisher hereby disclaims any responsibility for them.

Any people depicted in stock imagery provided by Getty Images are models, and such images are being used for illustrative purposes only. Certain stock imagery © Getty Images.

Scripture taken from the King James Version of the Bible.

ISBN: 978-1-6642-8041-0 (sc)
ISBN: 978-1-6642-8042-7 (hc)
ISBN: 978-1-6642-8040-3 (e)

Library of Congress Control Number: 2022918785

Print information available on the last page.

WestBow Press rev. date: 10/31/2022

Presented to:

_____

From:

_____

Date:

_____

DEDICATION

I dedicate this book to those of you who are hungry and thirsting after righteousness, to the ones who are seeking to understand the Bible, to the ones who have been struggling to know the truth, and to the ones who have said, "What am I missing?" To the ones who have a passion to do the will of God, I dedicate this book to you. I pray that you receive the message that Jesus wants you to know with joy as the revelational knowledge of these pages brings clarity to the questions you have had for a long time. I hope to encourage you to continue on this chosen path that leads us in the way that pleases God. As you read, may the gift on the inside of you be stirred to do what God has called you to do and to boldly proclaim the Word of God in your everyday life.

CONTENTS

INTRODUCTION

Today you have started an amazing journey into the kingdom of God. Expect to experience wonderful transformations with each chapter. The information in this book will impact your life forever. Each page will take you a step further on this royal path. Clear your mind and open your heart to receive the revealed knowledge that Jesus wants you to have. Enjoy, and be sure to smell the flowers along the way.

ACKNOWLEDGMENTS

A special tribute to missionary Irene May, my grandmother: thank you for planting a seed in my life so many years ago.

Also to missionary Luella Quinn, my mother: thank you for watering the seeds of faith that were planted.

Thank you, God, my God, for giving the increase.

Thank you, Jesus, my King, for all the love.

Thank you, Holy Spirit, my Comforter, for being with me.

To my husband, Terry Varnado; my children, Lukista and Cameron Jenkins, Jerry Walker, and James Walker III; and my grandchildren, Cali Rae Jenkins, Cason Jenkins, and James Walker IV.

Thank you to all of the ministers who teach the Gospel of the kingdom of God. Oh, how wonderful it is!

CHAPTER 1

A ROYAL PATH

On this royal path, let's look at some important details. In Matthew 3:13–15, Jesus left Galilee and came into Jordan, where John the Baptist was baptizing and preaching, saying, "Repent for the kingdom of God is at hand." Jesus approached John to be baptized. John tried to prevent Him, saying, "Instead of me baptizing you, I need you to baptize me." Jesus told John, "Permit it to be so now, for thus it is fitting for us to fulfill all righteousness."

One of the first things we can clearly see here on the royal path is the importance of following the road map. The road map is the Bible, which is the written Word of God. Right from the beginning, we see that Jesus did not take any shortcuts, nor did He think that this step wasn't important. It is very important for us to do exactly what the Bible says.

Each step in the right direction is crucial and necessary. Do not make excuses or change anything in the holy scripture. Just do exactly what it says

When you come to the knowledge of the truth, you must have a made-up mind to start correctly. If you begin to compromise in the beginning, it will cause you to get off the royal path. When you get off the path in this journey, the many distractions, deceptions, and dangers will cause you to stumble and lose your way. That is why you must read the Word of God for yourself and do what it says.

There may be times when someone else will try to tell you something different, but remember to always refer to what God has said in His Word, just like Jesus did when John told Him, "I need You, Jesus, to baptize me." Jesus stayed on the path and was baptized.

Some may think that baptism is not so important. Baptism is very important because it is in the Word of God, and even Jesus was baptized.

Some people may think that the thief who was saved on the cross was not baptized, but look at Mark 1:5: "And there went out unto him all the land of Judea, and they of Jerusalem, and were all baptized of him in the river Jordan, confessing their sins." *All* means "all." Jesus was also baptized before He was put on the cross.

Let's look at why baptism is important in the kingdom of God. In John 3:5, Jesus answered, "Verily, verily, I say unto thee, except a man be born of water and of the Spirit, he cannot enter into the kingdom of God." To enter into the kingdom of God, you must be born again. You can't enter the water in your mother's womb to be born again, but you can be submerged in the water of Mother Earth, come out, and be born again.

Sometimes we don't understand why He tells us to do certain things, but we trust Him. If He says, "Go wash your eyes in the pool," just go and do it. If He says, "Go straight" or "Turn right in two miles," just do what He has instructed you to do.

If He says, "Be baptized," then be baptized. Trust God's word and do what it says even when you don't understand the reason. God knows the process. You have never traveled this path before, but God created the path, and He knows what it will take for you to get to the place He has for you.

When you begin to do what He has told you to do in His word, you will experience some wonderful things God has just for you. It is in your obedience that you begin to see the wonderful transformations along the way. Things that you have never seen before will begin to unfold and be revealed. You will be able to smell the beautiful aroma of the flowers along this royal path.

In the book of Genesis, Adam and Eve did not obey God. They ate from the forbidden tree of the knowledge of good and evil, and they were kicked out of the garden of Eden. Afterward, Adam and Eve began to have children. In Genesis 4:1, Adam *knew* Eve, his wife, and she conceived. They were out of the will of God and in sin at this time. Therefore, all who were born in this way were born into sin. That is why we all must be born again.

Matthew 1:20 tells us that Jesus did not have a natural father and was conceived of the Holy Ghost. Mary's impregnation was a miraculous conception by the Holy Spirit. Therefore, Jesus was not born into sin, but He would take the sins of all people upon Himself.

In John 3:4, Nicodemus asked Jesus, "How can a man be born again?"

Jesus answered him in verse 5 by saying, "Except a man is born of water and spirit he can not enter into the Kingdom of God." We must do both—be born of *water and spirit*. Now you can see why baptism is so important and why Jesus told John it is fitting to fulfill all righteousness.

As soon as Jesus was baptized and came out of the water, the heavens opened up, and He saw the Spirit of God descending in the form of a dove. The dove landed on Him, and a voice from heaven said, "This is my son, whom I love, in Him I am well pleased" (Matthew 3:16–17). Both the water and the Spirit are described in this scripture when Jesus was baptized. When you do as the Bible says, you are doing what God wants you to do. You have a desire to do right. I encourage you to make the choice right now to take a step and follow the direction given to you in the Bible.

Whatever situation you may be dealing with at this time, go to the road map for direction and do what it says.

Proverbs 3:5–6 says, "Trust in the Lord with all thine heart; and lean not unto thine own understanding. In all thy ways acknowledge Him and He shall direct thy paths."

When the Bible says to trust God, trust God. When it says to forgive, then forgive. When it says to turn, you need to turn.

When it says to let go, you should let go. When it says to seek, you should seek. When it says not to love the things of the world, then don't love the things of the world. When it says to be either hot or cold, then be either hot or cold.

As you continue to take steps in the right direction, you will begin to see heaven opening up and the spirit of God dwelling with you. What a joy it is to experience the power of God working in your life. It is absolutely amazing.

In summary, here are some important things to remember while traveling on this royal path. Make up your mind to start doing right from the beginning. Do not compromise or think that things are not important, but do what the Word of God says to do. Jesus said that unless a man is born again of water and Spirit, he can't enter into the kingdom of God. You must be born of water and of Spirit, get baptized as Jesus was, and receive the Holy Spirit.

What touched your spirit while reading
chapter 1, "A Royal Path"?

CHAPTER 2

JESUS'S MESSAGE

ave you ever been around a person who has a passion for something? They love to talk about it, especially with someone who is really interested in what they are saying.

Jesus comes with an amazing love and compassion to share some valuable information. It is so profound for the ones who are interested that it will change their lives forever.

Jesus wants you to know about the kingdom of God. When Jesus began to preach, He preached about the kingdom of God, the kingdom of heaven. Matthew 4:17 tells us, "From that time Jesus began to preach, and to say, 'Repent, for the kingdom of Heaven is at hand.'" Matthew 4:23 says, "Jesus went about all Galilee, teaching in their synagogues, preaching the gospel of the kingdom, and healing all manner of sickness and all kinds of disease among the people." He preached and taught about the kingdom of God.

Jesus wants you to understand how everything relates to the kingdom of God. From the beginning of the Bible to the end, from Genesis to Revelation, it is all about God and His kingdom.

Jesus continued to teach and preach about the kingdom of God. In His first sermon, known as the Sermon on the Mount, in Matthew 5–7, Jesus sat on a mountain and told those listening how they should live according to the laws of the kingdom of God.

Then, in Matthew 8–9, He began to show forth the power of God by healing all manner of sickness and disease and raising the dead.

After Jesus taught the disciples about the kingdom, He sent them out and told them what they should preach.

In Matthew 10:7, He told the disciples, "And as you go, preach, saying, the kingdom of Heaven is at hand."

After Jesus's resurrection, He appeared to the disciples, telling them to remember the things that He had already commanded: to teach and preach the kingdom of God.

Matthew 28:18–20 (KJV) says, "And Jesus came and spake unto them, saying, all power is given unto me in heaven and in earth. Go ye therefore, and teach all nations, baptizing them in the name of the Father, and of the Son, and of the Holy Ghost: Teaching them to observe all things whatsoever I have commanded you."

All of Jesus's many parables tell us about the kingdom of God. In Matthew 13, Jesus tells the parable of the sower. A sower went out to sow some seeds. Some fell on stony places, where they did not have much earth, and they immediately sprang up because they had no depth. But when the sun came up, they were scorched, and because they had no roots, they withered. When He told them this parable of the sower, the disciples asked Jesus in verse 10 why He spoke in parables.

In Matthew 13:11, Jesus tells them, "Because it is given unto you to know the mysteries, of the kingdom of Heaven, but to them it is not given." So what was Jesus talking about in this parable? He was telling them about the mysteries of the kingdom of heaven, the kingdom of God. It was not given to the ones in the crowd; they were not interested in the things of the kingdom.

In Matthew 13:20–21, Jesus begins to explain the parable of the sower to the disciples, telling them that this is the person who hears the Word (the mysteries of the kingdom) and immediately receives it with joy; yet he has no root in himself so endures only for a while. For when tribulation or persecution arises because of the Word, immediately the person stumbles.

In Matthew 13:22, He said that some of the seeds fell among thorns, and the thorns sprang up and choked them. Jesus explains this to them, saying that this is the person who hears the Word (of the kingdom), but the cares of this world and the deceitfulness of riches choke the Word, and the person becomes unfruitful.

But others fell on good ground and yielded a crop; some a hundredfold, some sixty, and some thirty. In Matthew 13:23,

Jesus explains this and tells us that he who hears the Word and understands it is he who indeed bears fruit and produces. Some produce a hundredfold, some sixty, and some thirty.

When you hear the Word of the kingdom, you must be able to receive it in good ground. You must not have a stony heart, where it will not be able to take root. You must do the necessary things to be able to receive the Word of God.

You must be interested in the Word of God and ask questions like the disciples did until you understand it. And when tribulation and persecution come, don't give in but continue to do what God said in His word.

Do not care for the things of this world and do not be deceived by riches, because the evil one will try to deceive you and get you interested and caught up in the things of this world. Do not fall for it and allow the devil to shift your focus against what God has said. Some people are not willing to go through hard times and still do what is right; they will fall every time. But you have to have a made-up mind to believe God and do exactly what He said in order to enter into the things God has in store for you. He is not going to allow anyone in who will not follow the laws of His kingdom.

This is His territory, and He is gathering all the ones who really want to be part of a righteous kingdom.

When you hear the word of this glorious kingdom, seek to understand it, treasure it, and protect it. You will experience great joy in knowing that you are part of something so great. You will be part of an eternal kingdom where no one wicked can come in. You will be able to go through things and still do right to make sure you don't miss out on this. You will be so grateful and thankful to know that you will be in the place that God has prepared for you.

Jesus tells another parable, saying the kingdom of heaven is like a man who sowed good seed in his field, but while he slept, his enemies came and sowed tares, or weeds, among the wheat and went along his way. The servants ask the man if he wants them to go and pull them up, but the man says no, that they should just let them grow up together until harvesttime. "Then gather up all the tares and bind them up and burn them, and then gather the wheat and put in my barn" (see Matthew13:24–30). What a day this will be!

Wheat and tares look similar. Tares can sometimes be mistaken for wheat, but when harvesttime comes, the wheat stalks will have weight to them, which causes them to bow, but the tares have nothing in them and will be so light that they will be standing straight up. In the world, some people are like the tares, mixing with the people of God, but when it comes down to the end, they will not bow because they do not have what is required of them on the inside.

When the multitude was sent away, the disciples asked Jesus to explain to them the parable of the tares. In Matthew 13:36–43, Jesus answered, "The one who sowed the good seed is the Son of Man. The field is the world; the good seed are the children of the kingdom; but the tares are the children of the wicked one, the enemy who sows them is the devil. The harvest is the end of the world, and the reapers are angels. As the tares are gathered up and burned in the fire, so it will be at the end of the world. As John 8:44 lets us know, some people are not of God; they are of the devil.

> The Son of Man will send out His angels, and they will gather out of His kingdom all things that offend and them which do iniquity. And shall cast them into a furnace of fire: there shall be wailing and gnashing of teeth. Then shall the righteous shine forth as the sun in the kingdom of their father. Who hath ears to hear let him hear. (Matthew 13:41–43)

Jesus tells another parable in Matthew 13:31–32 in which the kingdom of heaven is "like to a grain of mustard seed," the least seed of all, but when it is grown, it becomes the greatest of the herbs. The kingdom of God started out small, with Jesus teaching the disciples. Jesus commanded the disciples to go and preach the kingdom of God to all nations.

In John 16:7, Jesus said, "Nevertheless I tell you the truth; it is expedient for you that I go away; for if I go not away; the Comforter will not come into you; but if I depart I will send Him unto you." Instead of the Holy Spirit being only in one, Jesus, He can be with the ones who receive Him all over the world. Jesus left and sent the Comforter, which is the Holy Spirit, and He will dwell with whoever accepts Jesus as their Lord and Savior and does what God has commanded in His word.

Jesus told them another parable: "The kingdom of heaven is like yeast that a woman took and mixed into about sixty pounds of flour until it worked all through the dough" (Matthew 13:33). This shows that the kingdom of God will spread throughout the world.

In Matthew 13:44, He says "The kingdom of heaven is like treasure hidden in a field. When a man found it, he hid it again, and then in his joy went and sold all he had and bought that field."

When you find the kingdom of God, it is the most wonderful, greatest treasure. There is no greater joy. Nothing else you have can ever compare. You will hide it in your heart so that no one and nothing can take it from you. You will be willing to give up everything to keep it. Romans 8:35 says, "Who shall separate us form the love of Christ? Shall tribulation, or distress, or persecution, or famine, or nakedness, or peril, or sword?" Then Romans 8:38–39 adds, "For I am persuaded, that neither death, nor life, nor angels, nor principalities, nor powers, nor things present, nor things to come, nor height, nor depth, nor any other creature, shall be able to separate us from the love of God, which is in Christ Jesus our Lord."

In Matthew 13:45–46, Jesus shares another parable with the disciples, saying, "Again the kingdom of heaven is like a merchant looking for fine pearls. When he found one of great value, he went away and sold everything he had and bought it."

In Matthew 13:47–50, Jesus told another parable about the kingdom of God: "The kingdom of heaven is like a net that was let down into the lake and caught all kinds of fish. When it was full, the fishermen pulled it up on the shore. Then they sat down and collected the good fish in baskets, but threw the bad away. This is how it will be at the end of the world. The angels will come and separate the wicked from the just and cast them into the furnace of fire, where there will be weeping and gnashing of teeth."

After sharing this parable about the fishers' net, Jesus asked the disciples "Have you understood all these things?" "Yes," the disciples replied. (Matthew 18:51)

Yes, the disciples understood what Jesus was telling them about the kingdom.

Then Jesus said to them, "Therefore every teacher of the law who has become a disciple in the kingdom of heaven is like the owner of a house who brings out of his storeroom new treasures as well as old" (Matthew 13:52). The kingdom of God is evident in the Old and New Testaments. The disciples began to share what they had just obtained and also to teach on the kingdom of God. Matthew was one of the disciples.

Matthew's writings tell us about the kingdom of God. He and other disciples wrote about how Jesus shared kingdom information with them.

You should now be able to see clearly what Jesus's message was. It was the kingdom of God. He really wants you to know about the kingdom of God, if you have a desire to know.

In the book of Acts, after Jesus was crucified and rose again, He appeared to the disciples and spent forty days telling them more things about the kingdom of God. Acts 1:3 says, "To whom also He shewed Himself alive by many infallible proofs, being seen of them forty days, and speaking of the things pertaining to the kingdom of God."

Matthew 23:13 tells us, "But woe unto you scribes and Pharisees, hypocrites! for you shut up the kingdom of heaven against men; for you neither go in your selves, neither suffer them that are entering to go in." The scribes and Pharisees, in today's world, are teachers and preachers who do not tell the people about the kingdom of God. These teachers and preachers do not go into the kingdom of God, and neither will they allow the people who are coming to them looking for the good news of the kingdom of God to enter in, because they will not even teach or preach about the kingdom of God.

But God is a righteous God, and everyone will be given the opportunity to hear about this gospel of the kingdom.

The disciples ask Jesus when the end would come, and He told them several things that would happen in the days leading up to the end. Then He specifically answered them in Matthew 24:14, saying "And this gospel of the kingdom shall be preached in all the world for a witness unto all nations; and then the end will come."

Some teachers and preachers may say that the gospel must be preached all over the world before the end will come, but they never say what gospel. Most never say the gospel of the kingdom must be preached. They may be talking about something else, but they need to say the gospel of the kingdom and teach and preach this because this is what Jesus's message is to us from God.

When kings in biblical days would send letters or messages to another king or another territory, the messengers would be very careful to protect the word from the king and to deliver it just as it was given. They were to reach their destinations just as they were originally written. These messages may have been inscribed on a stone or verbalized to the messengers; either way, the messengers had to make sure nothing about it changed or got broken or damaged. The messengers had to protect the messages and deliver them with the intent meant by the king because they knew that, if they didn't, they would face horrible consequences or even death.

Jesus said in Luke 4:43, "And He said unto them, I must preach the kingdom of God to other cities also: for therefore am I sent."

He said He was sent to preach the gospel of the kingdom.

What touched your spirit while reading
chapter 2, "Jesus's Message"?

CHAPTER 3
TREASURE HUNT

Imagine looking for something very valuable that has been hidden in a way that only the people who make an effort to seek and look for it will find it. On this treasure hunt, you have been given a set of clues and rules in order to find it. The one who hid it does not want just anybody to find it, but only people who believe and are obedient. So He tells you to seek. How do you begin? Yes, by following the clues and the rules that you have been given. In Matthew 6:33, Jesus tells us, "But seek ye first the kingdom of God and His righteousness and all these things will be added unto you." When the Bible says "seek ye first the kingdom of God and His righteousness," what should we do? Right, seek first the kingdom of God and His righteousness.

If someone asked you right now, "What is the kingdom of God," what would you tell them? Jesus told the disciples in

Matthew 10:7, "And as you go, preach the kingdom of heaven is at hand." This is the message that Jesus wanted the disciples to preach over all the nations. Jesus had taught them many things about the kingdom of God, and they asked Him to explain it to them when they didn't understand. They wanted to understand what Jesus was trying to tell them, and He made sure they understood. The disciples wrote it and shared it with us. You should want to learn and understand all about the kingdom of God.

When you seek something, you make an effort to look for it. You ask people who know about it, you read about it, and you study it. If you really want to know about something you are interested in, you will begin to search for and inquire about it. Once you find out and learn about the kingdom of God, you will know how the kingdom of God operates and know the righteousness of God. When you begin to understand His kingdom and His righteousness, you are obeying God. Then you will begin to say, "Not my will, Lord, but let thy will be done on earth as it is in heaven."

Many people have read this verse (Matthew 6:33) and never really thought about the first part of it. They are so focused on the last part of the verse that they will say it loudly: "And all these things will be added to you." They do not even do the first part, which says, "Seek ye first the kingdom of God and His righteousness."

The kingdom of God is the greatest treasure you will ever find. You have to desire to know and really want to seek and go looking for it to find it. When the disciples ask Jesus why

He speaks in parables, He answers them in Matthew 13:11–12: "Because it has been given to you to know the mysteries of the kingdom of heaven, but to them it has not been given. For whosoever has, to him more will be given, and he will have abundance; but whoever does not have, even what he has will be taken away from him."

If people are really not interested in the Word of the kingdom, when they do hear about the kingdom, they will not remember it or be able to use the information in times of tribulation because it did not take root in their hearts and will be taken away by the devil.

Matthew 13:19 tells us, "When anyone heareth the word of the kingdom, and understandeth it not, then cometh the wicked one, and catcheth away that which was sown in his heart." This is the person who received seed by the wayside.

The disciples had ears to hear (they had a desire to know) and were given more information when they asked. Matthew 5:6 says, "Blessed are those who hunger and thirst after righteousness for they shall be filled."

But many people in the crowd had different desires and did not have ears to hear. Whatever they did hear would be easily taken away by the devil, just like in the parable of the sower when some fell by the wayside. The disciples were focused on learning about the kingdom and asked Jesus questions so they could understand. In Matthew 13:16, Jesus told the disciples, "But blessed are your eyes, for they see: and your ears for they hear."

But many in the crowd were not focused on the things of

God. Matthew 13:15 says, "Their hearts have waxed cold and their ears had grown dull of hearing." They were not really interested in the things of God but more in the things of the world. They just wanted the "all these things will be added unto you" part without having to do the other part. The good hearts that chose to listen and understand will have these things added to them. When Jesus taught in a crowd, He did so in a way to hide this precious treasure. But the one who seeks the kingdom of God and its righteousness could find it.

Jesus tells us in Mathew 6:33 to seek ("seek ye first the kingdom"), so we have to seek. You have to inquire and have a desire and passion for it. Seeking takes effort. Because the kingdom of God is so precious, it will not be given to anyone who doesn't really care about the things of God.

And for the ones who are truly seeking, they will be able to see, hear, and understand what Jesus tells us about the kingdom of God. It is truly a blessing.

In Matthew 6:33, Jesus says, "But seek ye first the kingdom of God and His righteousness and all these things will be added unto you." Jesus said we should seek the kingdom of God first because He knows how vital it is for us to obtain the knowledge of the truth.

The kingdom was given to Adam and Eve. They had dominion over everything on earth. Adam and Eve did not ask for dominion. God put them in the garden and gave them instructions and a free will to choose what they wanted to do. They could choose to stay with God's word or listen to something else. Adam and Eve did not have to seek for the kingdom of God. It was just given to them. But they did not treasure it and keep it. They got distracted and deceived by the devil. They gave the devil what God had given them. They gave the devil power over them, when God had given them dominion and power over the devil.

Adam and Eve begin to listen to the devil and were interested in and entertained by what he said. They listened to the devil and did what he said. They obeyed the devil and that gave him power over themselves—because whomever you obey is whom you become a servant to. So now we have to desire and want this precious treasure. We have to seek for it, and when we find it, we will treasure it, protect it, and keep it. You should obey God and do what He says. When He says not to do something, you should not do it. There are sins of omission, which occur when you fail to do what God has told you to do. And there are sins of commission, which occur when you do what God has told you not to do.

Learning from Adam and Eve's story in the Bible, we can see what happened when they did not maintain the righteousness of God in the place that He had given them to rule. You should not listen to what the devil is trying to tell you because it is a trick, a lie. Uphold the Word of God in the place that He has placed you.

If you sincerely desire to know God, seek to know Him. Seek the kingdom of God and His righteousness. And you will find it because He will reveal the mysteries of the kingdom of God to you.

You can choose to be good or evil. He has given you all the

information you need to make a choice. If you accept Jesus and obey the things God has commanded you to do in His word, you will be part of the kingdom of God for eternity.

If you choose not to accept Jesus and not to do the things He has commanded, then you will be driven out of the kingdom and separated from God in eternal punishment. You can't be on both teams because one is wrong and one is right. There is no in between.

God wants no one to perish, He wants everyone to discover and find their way back to Him through Jesus Christ. He is a just God and has made sure everyone will be given the opportunity to be part of this righteous kingdom.

But they can be part of it if they accept Jesus and are willing to obey the laws of His righteous kingdom. You can't come into His place and His presence and do whatever you want. When Jesus was tempted in the wilderness by the devil, He fasted and stayed with the Word of God (Matthew 4:1–11).

"Ask and you shall receive, seek and you shall find, knock and the door will be open unto you" (Matthew 7:7–8). After seeking, you will find this wonderful, everlasting treasure that God has for you now and forever.

What touched your spirit while reading
chapter 3, "Treasure Hunt"?

CHAPTER 4

GOD'S KINGDOM

When looking at God's kingdom, you must consider two things: What is the kingdom of God? And what is His righteousness?

The kingdom of God is the territory that God reigns over and rules. He is over everything and everyone. He reigns because He created everything and everyone. He rules—He decides how He wants His kingdom to run and operate—because He created it. When people make things, they decide how they want those things to operate. The kingdom of God includes heaven and the earth because God created them both. When God created heaven and earth, He made the heavens the unseen spiritual realm, with transparent, invisible things and spirits.

God made the earth the seen physical realm, with water, land, grass, trees, animals, and humans. God created humans and gave them dominion over the fish of the sea, the fowl of the air, and everything living thing that moved upon the earth (Genesis 1).

God's throne is in heaven (Matthew 6:9). He is an unseen, invisible God. God is a Spirit. He reigns and rules over heaven and the earth. He gave humans dominion over the earth, under His rulership from heaven. Jesus said, "My kingdom is not of this world" (John 18:36).

When we accept Jesus and obey the laws that God has told us in His word, we can also say that our kingdom is not of this world.

That which is seen will pass away, but that which is unseen is will never die. Spirits live forever.

When people die, you remember their personalities and characters. You remember who they were and what they stood for. That is who they are, that is their spirit, and it will never die. I remember things my grandmother taught me when I was a child. She taught me to respect and fear God. She taught me that the Bible was God's word and that it was very important to obey.

In 2 Corinthians 4:18, we read, "While we look not at the things which are seen, but at the things which are not seen: for the things which are seen are temporal; but the things which are not seen are eternal."

Spirits are unseen and do not die; they live forever somewhere. That is why God will separate from Himself the evil, bad spirits and they will burn and be in torment forever.

Things that are unseen are more real and more powerful

than the things we can see. Thoughts that we can't see can produce things that we can see. People can have thoughts that we can't see, such as to build something or make a cake, but when they begin to put those thoughts into action, then we can see what they made.

There are some things we don't see, but they are real and so powerful that they can cause a work to be carried out.

Air, which we don't see, can enter our bodies upon inhalation and cause our lungs to expand, and we can see our bodies move. The wind that we can't see can cause things to move.

When people use cell phones, they can't see the signals going through the air, but something in the atmosphere that they can't see produces images that they can see and sounds they can hear.

When I was ministering at a prison, a young man told me that he did not believe in anything he couldn't see, and that is why he did not believe in God. By the time I got finished telling him about the other things he could not see, he understood and became a believer.

Spoken words are unseen, and they produce a spirit that goes out to do a work. You must be careful about what you say.

Words, when spoken, cause things to happen in the unseen realm that will later produce a work that will become evident in the seen realm: "And God said, let there be light, and there was light" (Genesis 1:3).

The words I spoke to that young man produced a thought that I could not see. That thought produced something that I could see. I saw his facial expression change in a way that said,

"There is a God." That was the point for him to start saying and doing things differently. He could no longer say he didn't believe in God because he didn't see Him.

That is why it is best to speak God's words and speak positively. Spoken words go out to produce works that are sometimes good and sometimes bad, depending on what words were spoken.

God's word does not return void; it goes out to accomplish the very thing it was sent out to do (Isaiah 55:11).

Jesus was the word. The word became flesh and was sent out to do a work, and He did not return to God void. He did what He was sent to do.

If a person says, "I can't do anything right" or "I can't ever get something good," if they say they are going to do something bad and they keep saying it, what do you think is going to happen? Yes, the very things that they are saying. Don't give the devil any grounds to steal, kill, and destroy your life, but speak positively and take action. Don't give the devil any rights to your body or your territory to come and do anything in your life.

When people begin to speak God's words instead of their own words, wishes, or wants, they will see transformation in their lives. Read 2 Corinthians 5:21. You can begin to say, "I am the righteousness of God through Jesus Christ. I can do all things through Christ that strengthens me" (Philippians 4:13). You can begin to say, "Not my will, Lord, but let thy will be done in my life."

When God speaks, it is done and it is eternal. Some people

may pray and say, "Speak, Lord." They better know what they are saying and be ready. When God fixes something, it is fixed. You don't have to be concerned about that anymore because it will be over and done.

I can remember times when God moved mightily in my life. Situations were taken care of better than I could have ever done or even imagined. When God works things out for you, you will know His power. Stop trying to do things your way, and just be led by God. Do what God says to do, and He will do what He said He would do.

In the Bible, we see examples when kings spoke and it became the law, and they do not change for anyone, not even themselves. When King Darius's men encouraged him to make a law that they knew Daniel would not obey—because Daniel believed in and worshipped only the true God and would not bow to any other—King Darius had to honor the law he had made because he had spoken it (Daniel 6).

The same is true of King Herod Antipas, the son of Herod the Great, who was pleasured by a girl's dancing and promised to give her whatever she asked for. She asked for the head of John the Baptist. Herod did not know that she would ask for the head of John, but he spoke the order and it was carried out (Mark 6:26).

When God told Adam and Eve to not eat from the tree of the knowledge of good and evil or they would surely die (Genesis 2:17), His Word was honored when they disobeyed. Adam and Eve died.

God even honors His own laws. Heaven is the unseen realm,

and earth is the physical, seen realm. No physical body can go into heaven. To be absent from the body is to be present with the Lord (2 Corinthians 5:8). Saints of God will meet the Lord in the air (1 Thessalonians 4:17).

We will be changed in a moment, in a twinkling of an eye (1 Corinthians 15:52). These physical bodies can't enter heaven. They will still be our bodies, but they will be changed.

The saints in the grave will rise first because their spirits will already be in heaven, but they will come back with Jesus. When He comes with them, they will be rejoined with their bodies and be changed, and the ones who remain will be caught up, and we all will be changed and given incorruptible bodies.

Likewise, spirits can't dwell (stay for a long period of time) on earth without bodies. They can visit, but they can't dwell unless they are in a physical composition, observable bodies.

Spirits go to and fro trying to enter people so they can stay on earth instead of going to be tormented early, before the appointed time set by God. God has a set a time for them to begin being tormented forever. They are already judged. When angels were deceived by Lucifer and sided with him in heaven, they became demons. They committed sins in the spiritual realm, their punishment was given, and it is eternal. Spirits are in an eternal state of being. Blasphemy against the Holy Spirit will not be forgiven (Matthew 12:31). The Holy Spirit is God's Spirit. When a person talks badly about Him, they will not do anything He says to do or accept Him into their lives. How can they be forgiven when they are keeping Him away? That is their choice, to deny and not to believe, which causes them to say profane things against the Holy Spirit. If they are blaspheming Him, they are surely not going to receive Him. They definitely will not let Him come in and sanctify and seal them. They are denying Him access. The Holy Spirit is the last part of the Trinity to come. First, it was God talking to Adam and Eve and the prophets, then Jesus came, and now we are in the dispensation of the Holy Spirit. Nothing else is coming. This is the last chance they have, and some continue to deny Him.

God gave us the truth, a choice, and a lifetime to make a choice. So everyone can have the opportunity to avoid eternal punishment.

God carries out His spoken words, His laws. Please don't think He will change them for you or anyone else. He does not even change them for Himself. God upholds His own laws. He goes through all the necessary steps in the process to do things right according to the laws of His kingdom.

That is why God created Himself a body, Jesus, so He would be able to dwell (stay for a period of time) on earth for a while and tell us the gospel truth, which is the good news, of the kingdom of God. This shows us God honoring and keeping His own rules because He is a Spirit and spirits are not to dwell on earth without a body. Heaven is the unseen, spiritual realm, and earth is the seen, physical realm. God is a Spirit.

Jesus sacrificed His life so we can have a *chance* to be partakers of the kingdom of God. God spoke and told Adam and Eve to not eat from the tree of the knowledge of good and evil or they would surely die, so in Jesus dying for all of us, we can see God honoring His Word, His laws. This is God honoring His laws, His spoken Word, in a way that He can save us. Jesus died for all humankind, past, present, and future. Jesus's being that once-and-for-all sacrifice was God's plan to redeem humanity back unto Himself, back to being part of His kingdom, and back to the purpose which He created humans for, in the place where He placed them.

God gave us all a choice. We can make the choice to believe and accept Jesus's redemptive work or not. This is another way God honors His word and His laws. Believing is not forced upon us; some choose to believe and obey, and some don't. Blessed are those who believe. John 20:29 says, "Jesus saith unto him, Thomas, because thou hast seen me, thou hast believed: blessed are they that have not seen, and yet have believed."

When God created man and woman, He gave them dominion over the earth and a choice. Today we can choose to receive God's spirit through the redemptive work of Jesus and allow Him to do His work on earth.

God uses people to carry out His work on the earth. The Holy Spirit, which is God's Spirit, can live inside the ones who accept Jesus as their Lord and Savior and obey. God gave humans dominion over the earth. God will not do anything on earth without a person allowing Him to use his or her body. Whenever people allow God to work through them to accomplish His will on earth, this shows God honoring the laws of His kingdom, and it also shows humans in right relationship with God under His rulership and giving God access to do what He will on earth. "Our Father which art in heaven hallowed be thy name.... Let thy will be done on earth as it is in heaven"

(Matthew 6:9, 10). We can say, "Lord, not my will, but let thy will be done."

We can see in the Bible God asking people to do things. In Exodus 9:1, He tells Moses to go tell Pharaoh to "let my people go." And in Jonah 3:2, God tells Jonah go to Nineveh and warn the people to turn from their wicked ways, to turn from their lifestyle.

Spirits go to and fro seeking a body to enter. Even God's Spirit, the Holy Spirit, seeks someone through whom He can show Himself strong.

Spirits will even go into animals until they find people who will let them in. In Matthew 8:28–34, evil spirits came out of a man and asked to go into some nearby pigs so they could stay for a while longer on earth and not be tormented before it was time.

They are trying harder and harder because they know their time is almost up. In Numbers 22:21–39, Balaam's donkey spoke to him until Balaam was able to see the angel in his path, and then the Lord spoke to Balaam.

Evil spirits also seek people they may enter into to cause them to disobey God. They want to get into people's bodies because that is the only way they can do anything. Each person must choose whether to allow his or her body to be used. A spirit on earth without a body will just hang out in the air, helpless for a short time as it tempts people in all kind of ways to get them to listen and let them into their bodies.

In Genesis 3:1–7, the evil spirit, the devil, tempted Adam and Eve. He could not do anything to them: he could not kill them or curse them. The only thing he could do was tempt them to do what God said not to do. He knew that if they broke the law, God will carry out what He said he would do. Adam and Eve would be kicked out, just as the devil was. When they received the lying spirit into themselves, into their minds, they did an evil work and disobeyed God.

Imagine a spirit of hatred was out in the air. It could do no harm if no one allowed it to enter, but if a person allowed that spirit to enter into them, then it could hurt or even kill someone.

Remember, God is ruler over all. God is all powerful. Spirits are given only a portion of power, God allows for reasons that only God knows. It is the infinite wisdom and sovereignty of God. Spirits can't do anything or even tempt anyone unless God allows them to. They must have permission from the Almighty God. When the devil thinks he is doing something underhanded, God already knows and has allowed it to prove something or for a reason and purpose that God knows.

This is true of any spirit, any part of the unseen spiritual realm. This is true of all spirits, whether they be spirits of hatred, lust, greed, envy, or pride. Be aware of the devil's devices, especially the things you can't see. If a spirit is not lining up with God's word, do not give it access. In 2 Corinthians 2:11, we read, "Lest Satan should get an advantage of us: for we are not ignorant of his devices." The devil did not use a knife or gun on Adam and Eve; he used words, unseen words.

You must protect the entryways into your body. The devil will try to enter any way he can. Be aware of what your eyes see. Do not let anything enter that is out of the will of God. If something on television is not in line with God's word and is piercing your thoughts and feelings in a way that is against what God said in His Word, stop watching it. The lust of the eyes will cause you to act in a way that is contrary to the will of God.

If words or music cause you to think wrong thoughts and do wrong things, stop listening to it. Get away from people whose talk is negative and contrary to the Word of God. Protect your ears from things that are not right.

If a certain perfume or cologne creates a desire for someone other than your spouse, do not entertain, flirt, or do anything wrong. Be aware of the devil's subtle ways.

If you smell something that compromises your mental status and is being misused to control the body and keep you unaware of some things, this is a trick of the devil. The same goes for touch and taste. Don't be deceived by the devil. He has subtle ways to enter and lead you to say or do things that God does not want you to say or do. Be aware that the devil is trying to slip in all the time, trying to keep your mind off God. It's no wonder that some signs say "wine and spirits." But there is a good spirit, God's Spirit, which is the Holy Spirit, and instead of hatred it produces the fruit of love. Instead of confusion and disobedience, it produce peace and obedience to God's word.

Jesus tells us this is why he came to tell us about God's kingdom. Luke 4:43 says, "And He said unto them, I must preach the kingdom of God to other cities also: for therefore am I sent." He was sent to do what? Yes, He was sent to preach the kingdom of God. This is so amazing. Thank you, Jesus, for sacrificing your life for us so we can have a chance to be part of this great kingdom of God.

Over the years, the devil has put up so many distractions that people have lost the knowledge of the kingdom of God and His righteousness. So many false prophets teach everything except the gospel of the kingdom of God.

Jesus had to sacrifice His life to make it possible for us to even have a chance to get back in a right relationship with God after Adam and Eve disobeyed. We now have a chance to accept Jesus and do what God has commanded in His word so that we can be reunited with God through Jesus. He was with Adam and Eve before they sinned, talking with them; they were over the earth, and He was over them.

In the Old Testament, the Israelites asked for a man to be their king instead of knowing that God was their King. They should have acknowledged Him as King. God is over all, and He has given Jesus authority as our King.

God wishes that no one would perish. He wants everyone to repent and be saved from eternal punishment. But He will not break the law of His kingdom. This is His righteousness. God is a righteous God.

His kingdom will be one with order and obedience unto Him on the wonderful new earth. Everyone who makes the choice to believe in Jesus and do what God said can live in God's kingdom under His ultimate authority from heaven. Revelation 21:1–2 says, "And I saw a new heaven and a new earth: for the first heaven and the first earth was passed away; and there was no more sea. And I John saw the holy city, New Jerusalem, coming down from God out of heaven, prepared as a bride adorned for her husband." This right here is so beautiful. This is the place God is preparing for us. You don't want to miss out on this.

Do whatever you can now. Do all you can now—suffer if you must—but do not miss out on this.

Think of everything you have done wrong, even when you were a child but knew better. Ask God to forgive you.

Now think back to everything that others have done wrong to you. If you can reach them, have you told them that you forgive them? Have you forgiven them? If you have not forgiven, then the things for which you ask God to forgive you are not forgiven. Matthew 6:15 says, "If you forgive not men of their trespasses, neither will your Father forgive your trespasses." This is how the laws of the kingdom will work. You must believe and obey. Do not be deceived: the unrighteous shall not inherit the kingdom of God. In 1 Corinthians 6:9–10, we read, "Know ye not that the unrighteous shall not inherit the kingdom of God? Be not deceived: neither fornicators, nor idolaters, nor adulterers, nor effeminate, nor abusers of themselves with mankind, nor thieves, nor covetous, nor drunkards, nor revilers, nor extortioners, shall inherit the kingdom of God."

If you have difficulty obeying anything what God has told us to do in His word, sincerely ask Him to help you. You will begin to see the Holy Spirit work in your life. God will not break His laws for Himself. He would not break them for Adam and Eve. Don't think He is going to break them for you, but He will help you.

You must believe and obey. Believe God and accept Jesus as your Lord and Savior. If He is Lord over you, you will do what He says. If you are not seeing God manifest in your life, begin to obey His laws.

If the Word of God says to do a certain thing and then something will happen, don't do something different and expect His word to change. When you do what God said to do, He will do what He said He would do.

If God does not do some things that you think He should do, understand that there is something that you don't know. He knows what is best for us more than we do. I trust God.

Some things happen for a purpose that God knows. Maybe we are holding onto something we don't need or we need to do something to get us to a place within the laws of the kingdom so we will not block anything God has for us according to His Word. God will not reveal some things to us for various reasons; only He knows. His wisdom is infinite, and He is sovereign.

Look at the Hebrew boys in the fiery furnace. Daniel 3:17–18 says, "If it be so, our God whom we serve is able to deliver us from the burning fiery furnace, and He will deliver us out of thine hand, o king. But if not, be it known unto thee, O king, that we will not serve thy gods, nor worship the golden image which thou hast set up." In other words, even if God doesn't save us for a reason only He knows, we know that He can. So it really doesn't matter to me; I'm staying with God. He can choose to deliver me or not. I'm staying with God. I trust God.

God is seeking to restore the original relationship with humans through Jesus. But we must seek and understand His kingdom and His laws. The kingdom does not operate by feelings or emotions but by the laws that govern it.

In the book of Genesis, God gave Adam and Eve all the herbs that yield seeds, every green herb, and every tree whose fruit yield seeds to be food for them. Also, He gave them every beast of the earth, every bird of the air, and everything that creeps on the earth that has life for food. He commanded them to not eat from or even touch the tree of knowledge of good and evil, but they were deceived by the devil to disobey God. They ate from the tree that God had told them not to eat from or touch. They did not keep the Word of God.

When the devil was trying to tempt Jesus in the wilderness, Jesus stayed with the Word of God. He did not negotiate or compromise any part of the Word of God. He spoke the Word just as it was and did not listen to or fall for what the devil was tempting Him with.

The Word of God is so important. You must read, understand, and know the Word of God. You must not let it fall by the wayside or on a stony heart. Receive it on good ground and hide it in your heart so that, when the enemy comes to you, you will be able to speak it and not sin against God. That is why, in every situation, you must refer to the Word of God and do exactly what it says.

God gave Adam and Eve the law, but they broke the law and they suffered the consequences. God obeys and honors His own laws.

When Adam and Eve disobeyed, God covered them with skin and put them out of the Garden of Eden so they would no longer have access to the tree of life and live forever.

Adam and Eve are no longer alive; they have surely died, just as the Word of God said. In the book of Genesis, we see that the devil lied and tricked them, telling them that they would not surely die, but they did surely die. They would have lived forever, but after they sinned, they started to die. When a person's punishment does not come quickly, some think they have gotten away with their sin. But that is not so—their punishment will come.

When God covered them with skins, this started the sacrificial system that would cover humans' sins for a while and give them a chance to repent. Nevertheless, sacrificing animals was not a forever solution.

Animals were sacrificed to atone for sins until Jesus, who made the choice not to sin and was without sin, sacrificed his life for the sins of all.

Romans 5:12 says, "Therefore, just as sin entered the world through one man and death through sin, and in this way death passed upon all men, for that all have sinned." Romans 5:19 says, "For as by one man's disobedience many were made sinners, so by the obedience of one shall many be made righteous."

Jesus had to come and be our once-and-for-all sacrifice so that we would have a chance to be a part of the kingdom. John 14:6 says, "Jesus saith unto him, I am the way, the truth and the light: no man cometh unto the Father, but by me." This is the only way we can get back into a right relationship with God, back to the place of obedience with God in the Garden of Eden, having dominion over the things He placed us over. This is the message Jesus was telling us: God is the only true, living, righteous, all-powerful God. He has given Jesus authority as our King.

Many have been deceived into veering away from the Word of God. Over the years, many have listened to the devil's lies and twisting of the truth. When people begin to listen to the devil's lies and choose to not speak boldly the word that God has given them, they will become distracted and enticed by what they are hearing and seeing.

Being interested in something other than the word that was given by God will cause you to be deceived. Adam and Eve began to do the very thing that God said not to do or even touch because they allowed themselves to fall for a lie. They became interested and wanted to try it.

He created us and gave us a choice. This is why the tree of the knowledge of good and evil was there and the commandment was given. If you have to trick or force a person into loving you, it is not love.

Tell them the truth and let them decide. This is what God did. He told them the truth and let them decide. We can clearly see and have come to the realization that we are in a fallen world.

Some people may wonder how God could let all these bad things happen. One of the laws God spoke was, "Let them have dominion." God gave people dominion over the earth. So don't blame God. God honors and does not even break His own laws. But He has a plan within His laws to save us.

That is why He had to come through man to dwell on earth. He created Himself a body, Jesus, so He could do things on earth and still uphold what He had spoken, the law He had given for humans to have dominion over the earth. God is the creator of everything and can do anything, but He chooses to do right. God is a righteous God, and He follows the laws of His kingdom.

The Bible gives examples of this in earthly kings. When they say something, they uphold it no matter what.

God uses people to accomplish His will on earth; that is why we were created. We were created to have dominion over the earth and to keep order under His guidance. God has not taken back His word. God honors and upholds His word. I answer questions and explain further in my conferences when people ask questions regarding this. Genesis 1:28 says, "And God blessed them, and God said unto them, Be fruitful, and multiply, and replenish the earth, and subdue it: and have dominion over the fish of the sea and over the fowl of the air, and over every living thing that moveth upon the earth."

Similar to the natural laws on earth, if you disobey God's laws, consequences will follow. God is building His kingdom with only people who choose and want to be part of it and obey its laws. As for others who do not choose to obey, they will suffer the consequences of not obeying and be driven out of His presence forever—because spirits live forever. That is why the choices you make will determine where you will spend eternity. Do not allow yourself to be tricked. God has told us what to do and what not to do. This is who we are; we are His.

He created us, and we can trust Him. He created us to be part of Him and His family. We are kings, queens, princes, and princesses. We are royalty. We are a royal priesthood, chosen by God.

Some people think that, if they believe in Jesus, that is all they have to do to be saved. Now, we know that works alone will not save us, but it is only by the blood of Jesus that we can even have a chance to be saved. There is nothing that we can ever do to be saved without God's grace. To think that all you have to do is to believe and nothing else when the Bible has told you differently means you are not seeing and hearing everything clearly.

We must do both, believe and do what He says. When you believe and accept Jesus as your Lord and Savior, you are accepting His rulership and choosing to obey the laws of the kingdom. The word *lord* means "master," "ruler," "one who has authority over another." To accept Him as Lord is saying that you will obey Him and will be under His authority.

Luke 6:46 says, "But why do you call me 'Lord, Lord' and do not do the things which I say?" If you don't obey Him, you have not accepted Him.

Matthew 7:21 says, "Not everyone who says to me, 'Lord, Lord' shall enter the kingdom of heaven, but he who does the will of my Father in heaven."

To enter the kingdom of God, it takes both: you must accept Christ and obey His word.

In Acts 22:10, Saul asked, "What shall I do, Lord?" Jesus told Saul to go into the city and await instructions on what to do. Then, in Acts 22:16, the Lord sent Ananias to tell Saul to be baptized and wash his sins away. That is doing something.

Romans 10:9 begins with, "That if thou shall confess with thy mouth." That is doing something that the Word of God told you to do. Then it says, "and shalt believe in thine heart that God hath raised Him from the dead, thou shalt be saved." When you believe and accept Jesus as your Lord and Savior, you are accepting His rulership. You are agreeing to obey what the Word of God says.

To enter the kingdom of God, you must do both—believe and accept Christ—by obeying the Word of God. You should be baptized and do the other things He has commanded you.

Works alone do not save us. Believing alone does not save us. It takes a willing heart to do both.

When Paul and Silas were brought out of prison by one of the guards, the guard asked them, "… Sirs, what must I do to be saved? And they said, Believe on the Lord Jesus Christ, and thou shalt be saved, and thy house. And they spake unto him the word of the Lord, and to all that were in his house. And he took them, the same hour of the night, and washed their stripes; and was baptized, he and all his, straightway" (Acts 16:30–33).

Hebrews 11:6 tells us, "But without faith it is impossible to please Him: for he that comes to God must believe that He is, and that He is a rewarder of them that diligently seek Him."

What touched your spirit while reading
chapter 4, "God's Kingdom"?

GOD'S SOVEREIGN WILL

CHAPTER 5

f you could do whatever you wanted, how bad would you be? Or, should I say, how *good* would you be? God is sovereign and can do whatever He wants to do, but He chooses to do good and not evil. God is a righteous God who does things according to His will for a good purpose. He is independent and governs Himself. No one is above God. He has supreme authority over all, with unlimited power and authority.

Look at how Nebuchadnezzar says it in Daniel 4:34–35:

And at the end of the days I Nebuchadnezzar lifted up mine eyes into heaven, and mine understanding returned unto me, and I blessed the most high, and I praised and honoured Him that liveth for ever, whose dominion is an everlasting dominion, and His kingdom is from generation to generation. And all the inhabitants of the earth are reputed as nothing: and He doeth according to His will in the army of heaven, and among the inhabitants of the earth: and none can stay His hand, or say into him, What doest thou?

God has supreme power over all. He has given people a choice to be in His kingdom or not. No one will reign over God.

When you want to be in His kingdom, there are laws you must follow. Anyone who owns something should have rules so that no one else can come in and take over.

Some ask, "If God has all power, why does He let bad things happen?" It's because He gave humankind dominion over earth, so they are responsible for the condition it's in. God did not change His word or take it back; He still honors His word.

He upholds His laws that He has spoken, and He goes through the necessary steps to do things the right way. He will not break them or dishonor His word.

Some may have wondered why God doesn't just get rid of the devil and destroy him. The devil is an evil spirit, and spirits live forever. That is why the evil spirits will be separated from God and tormented forever at the appointed time set by God. God is using the devil for other purposes known by God, but at the appointed time that only God knows, he will be tormented forever along with those who chose to follow him.

God allows him to tempt people, like he did Jesus, Job, Abraham, and others. The devil means the temptation for bad, but God means it for good. Exodus 16:4 says, "Then said the Lord unto Moses, Behold, I will rain bread from heaven for you; and the people shall go out and gather a certain rate every day, that I may prove (test) them, whether they will walk in my law, or no."

Some may ask why some people are born sick or why bad things happen to babies. God has reasons for everything He does or allows to happen according to His Word and laws. He chooses not to reveal some things for reasons only He knows. John 9:2–3 says, "And His disciples asked Him, saying, Master, who did sin, this man, or his parents, that he was born blind? Jesus answered, neither hath this man sinned, nor his parents: but that the works of God should be made manifest in him."

Before the fall of humankind, Adam and Eve experienced only good. After they ate from the forbidden tree, humankind was opened to experience both good and evil. Did roses always have thorns? The condition of the earth is getting worse. The sin of people is bringing destruction upon themselves.

Matthew 24:22 says, "And except those days shall be shortened, there should be no flesh be saved: but for the elect's sake those days shall be shortened."

No one can question what God does. You should trust Him in all that He does. Even before you were formed in your mother's womb, He created you to do a specific work for Him. He gave you the amount of time you need to complete the task. Everyone was given life. Although the lengths of those lives are different, they are according to what He purposed for them.

If you don't know what purpose God called you to do, just look at the position into which you were born or are in now. Every instance is an opportunity to serve God. Are you a husband, brother, father, friend, employee, son, sister, wife, daughter, mother, niece, nephew, neighbor, and so on? Be the best one you can be. Are you in a position as a teacher, nurse, store clerk, cook, leader, helper, and so on? Be the best one you can be. Have you been chosen to do a specific task? In all things you do, do them as a service unto the Lord.

Receive the Holy Spirit. Listen to and be led by the Holy Spirit. The Holy Spirit was sent to earth to be with us to help us reach a place in our lives that God has chosen for us. The Holy Spirit will lead, guide, teach, and comfort you.

God is sovereign, and He has given everyone a purpose according to His will. God's purpose and will for your life is going to be done. God's Word goes out, and it does not return void; but it produces that which it was sent out to do. If people do not line up with God's calling on their lives, God's purpose will still be done. Depending on the choices people make, they will end up on one side of that purpose or the other. Consider the story of Sampson. Destined by God, Sampson was created with strength to carry out a work. The work that he was sent to do was completed, but because he got caught up, enticed, and tricked by what he was sent to destroy, Sampson was also destroyed in the process. But the work was carried out. What God created you to do will be done, but where will you end up in the process?

God chooses to keep some things from us for a reason. If people knew when they were going to die or when Jesus was coming back, they would try to wait and get saved just before they died or just before He returned.

Think about a person who is faithful only when his or her spouse is around. Pretending to be faithful is not being faithful. God does not want this type of relationship. When He returned to Adam and Eve, He saw that they had not been faithful and had sinned. He is giving you a chance now to make up your mind. You are either all in or all out. You are either hot or cold.

All things will work together for the good of those who are called according to His purpose.

God will not tell us some things because, if we knew them, we may do some things differently. If a person knew he or she would live to be twenty years old or ninety-eight years old, that knowledge might change how he or she lived life. Likewise, if people knew when Jesus would return, they might behave differently at that time. God does not want our choices to be based on these things. He wants them to be pure. He knows and allows us to see what is in our hearts, giving us a chance and a choice to repent or not. Some things are not revealed for other purposes that only God knows.

He knows what is best for us. He knows what is needed to bring us to a place that He has purposed for us.

God created all things for His will and to fulfill His good purpose. You have been created for a purpose that God wanted to you to carry out.

Revelation 4:11 says, "Thou art worthy, O Lord, to receive glory and honour and power: for thou hast created all things, and for thy pleasure they are and were created." God wants us to praise Him because it shows Him that we understand and see all the things He has done for us, all the things He went through just to save us and to give us another chance.

God deserves our praise, and we praise Him to show that we reverence Him and that we are truly thankful for the things

He has done to give us the opportunity to be restored back to Him. If God had not given us His grace and His mercy, we would have been in eternal, everlasting torment. He deserves all the praise.

How can we give God praise and glory? We who worship God must worship Him in Spirit and in truth. We can outwardly worship and praise and show Him that we love him. We can lift our hands in worship, we can verbally praise him, and we can sing songs that glorify Him.

Luke 9:26 says, "For whosoever shall be ashamed of me and of my words, of him shall the son of man be ashamed, when he shall come in his own glory, and in his Father's, and of the holy angels." Some people have relationships with people but are ashamed for others to know about them. They never want anyone to know they are in relationships with these people. They don't want anyone to see them together. They want to see them only at night or in secret. Do not be ashamed to acknowledge God and tell others about Him. You can't use God; either you are with Him or you are not.

In Matthew 25:1, Jesus tells a parable:

> Then shall the kingdom of heaven be likened unto ten virgins, which took their lamps, and went forth to meet the bridegroom. And five of them were wise, and five were foolish. They that were foolish took their lamps, and took no oil with them. But the wise took oil in their vessels with their lamps. While the bridegroom tarried,

they slumbered and slept. And at midnight there was a cry made, Behold, the bridegroom cometh; go ye out to meet him. Then all those virgins arose, and trimmed their lamps. And the foolish said into the wise, Give us of your oil; for our lamps are gone out. But the wise answered, saying, Not so; lest there be not enough for us and you: but go ye rather to them that sell, and buy for yourselves. And while they went to buy, the bridegroom came; and they that were ready went in with him to the marriage: and the door was shut. Afterward came also the other virgins, saying, Lord, Lord, open to us. But he answered and said, Verily I say unto you, I know you not.

Another parable in Matthew 25:14–15 says, "For the kingdom of heaven is as a man travelling into a far country, who called his own servants, and delivered unto them his goods. And unto one he gave five talents, to another two, and to another one; to every man according to his several ability; and straightway took his journey." Matthew 25:20–30 reads,

And so he that had received five talents came and brought other five talents, saying, Lord, thou deliveredst unto me five talents: behold, I have gained beside them five talents more. His lord said unto him, Well done, thou good and faithful servant: thou hast been faithful over a few things, I will make thee ruler over many things: enter thou into the joy of thy lord. He also that had received two talents came and said, Lord, thou deliveredst unto me two talents: behold, I have gained two other talents beside them. His lord said unto him, well done, good and faithful servant; thou hast been faithful over a few things, I will make thee ruler over many things: enter thou into the joy of thy lord. Then he which had received the one talent came and said, Lord, I knew thee that thou art an hard man, reaping where thou hast not sown, and gathering where thou hast not strawed: And I was afraid, and went and hid thy talent in the earth: lo, there thou hast that is thine. His lord answered and said unto him, Thou wicked and slothful servant, thou knewest that I reap where I sowed not, and gather where I have not strawed: Thou oughtest therefore to have put my money to the exchangers, and then at my coming I should have received mine own with usury. Take therefore the talent from him, and give it unto him which hath ten talents. For unto every one that hath shall be given, and he shall have abundance: but from him that hath not shall be taken away even that which he hath. And cast ye the unprofitable servant into outer darkness: there shall be weeping and gnashing of teeth.

The servants did not know when their lord would come back. While he was gone, they may have thought he would not return. Day after day went by, and one day the man returned.

Do not think that your talent or assignment doesn't matter or that your gift is too small. Be fruitful and multiply what God has given you.

It is important to God. In the story of the talents, the master had been gone so long that the servants did not know when he would return. One buried his talent and did not do anything.

Just imagine if someone left you in charge of their property, and all you did was eat and enjoy their property. You didn't do anything to keep it looking good. You didn't keep the lawn, you did not clean up, you didn't keep animals out, you let dust pile up, and when the owner came back to his property, you told him, "Here it is. I didn't bother it or do anything to it." Can you imagine the owner's response upon seeing his property?

Well, that is how some people have messed up their lives and the things of which God put them in charge. We are God's property and He gave us dominion, but He also gave us a choice to decide what we want to do with our lives and the things He has put us over. Everyone has been given talents, each one of different amounts, according to their ability.

Your life is a gift from God. No one knows the day or the hour when Jesus will return.

The time for Jesus to return is closer than it has ever been. Although it has been a long time, we are in the last days. First was God talking with Adam and Eve, then Jesus came, and now we are in the dispensation of the Holy Spirit. Nothing else is coming. The Father, the Son, and the Holy Spirit. These are the last days. And we are closer today than we have ever been to Jesus's returning. The condition of the world today is the sign Jesus told the disciples to watch for when they asked Him when the end would come. He told them the things that would happen. In Matthew 24:14, He tells them, "And this gospel of the kingdom shall be preached in all the world for a witness unto all nations; and then shall the end come." When the gospel of the kingdom is preached all over the world, then the end will come. Preaching is going out all over the world, but is it the gospel of the kingdom?

God will give everyone a chance to know about His kingdom. He is a righteous God. God is love. Love God, love yourself, and love others. John 13:35 says, "By this shall all men know that ye are my disciples, if ye have love one to another."

What an awesome, loving, righteous, true, living, and all-powerful God we serve. He is a sovereign God.

What touched your spirit while reading
chapter 5, "God's Sovereign Will"?

CHAPTER 6

THE HOLY SPIRIT

When people pass away, they are no longer here on earth. Their spirits are separated from their bodies, but their spirits are still very much alive. We can no longer see them, but we know who they were and what they stood for. Their spirits describe them.

God's Spirit is unseen, describing who He is and what He stands for. God's Spirit is now available to dwell in believers' bodies on earth when they receive Him. They begin to have the characteristics of their Father, His Spirit. They begin to produce the fruit of the Spirit. The Holy Spirit is God's Spirit. God is the unseen, invisible, living God. He is God the Father, God the Son, and God the Holy Spirit. The three are one. For an example, look at H_2O: it can be vapor, ice, and water. The Holy Spirit is not a mist, vapor, or liquid, but He is the Spirit of God.

In the beginning, it was God talking with Adam and Eve.

It was God who dwelt on the inside of Jesus. It is God's Spirit, which is the Holy Spirit, that is dwelling within the believers on the earth today. He has never left us or forsaken us.

In John 16:7, Jesus says, "Nevertheless I tell you the truth, it is expedient for you that I go away: for if I go not away the Comforter will not come unto you; but if I depart, I will send Him unto you."

The Holy Spirit is the last part of the Trinity to come before Jesus returns. God, Jesus, and the Holy Ghost (Holy Spirit)—no one else is coming. We are in the last days before Jesus returns. The Holy Spirit is here with the saints today.

The Holy Spirit will bear witness to Jesus. "He shall glorify me: for He shall receive of mine; and shall shew it unto you. All things that the Father has is mine: therefore said I, that He shall take of mine, and shall shew it unto you" (John 16:14–15).

In John 16:8–14, Jesus tells us that, when the Comforter comes, He will reprove the world of sin, of righteousness, and of judgment. The Holy Spirit will reprove the world. He will convict you of your sins. He will make you aware of the things of God. You should repent of your sins and continue to be led by the Holy Spirit. He helps you and gives you the knowledge and power to do right. We don't have the power to keep ourselves. We can allow the Holy Spirit to govern us because we give Him the authority to do so. When we allow Him to lead and guide us in the Word of God, we will continue to be obedient. Jude, verse 24, says, "Now unto Him who is able to keep you from falling, and present you faultless before the presence of His glory with exceeding joy." The Holy Spirit will take you through the process of sanctification in all areas in your life. He will help you. He will guide you and move things out of your way so you will not stumble.

The Holy Spirit will give you gifts. They are —the fruit of the Spirit. You will see that, in your life, you will have love, joy, peace, patience, kindness, goodness, faithfulness, gentleness and self-control (Galatians 5:22–23). These gifts will help on our journey.

God tempts no one, but the Holy Spirit will test you. *Tempt* and *test* are not the same. Whenever you are going through situations, God means them for good. God want to see you uphold His word and do good, but the devil means them for bad and wants to tempt you to disobey God.

In life, we take tests that make sure we know how to do things correctly and how to handle situations. I earned my degree in nursing, but I could not practice as a registered nurse until I passed the required licensure test. When you pass the test, it will set you apart, and you will be able to carry out the work you were designed to carry out.

God allows people to go through different types of tests for different purposes. For example, marriage and relationships will test and try you. Can I get an amen?

Before Jesus began His ministry, He was led into the wilderness by the Spirit to be tempted by the devil (Matthew 4:1). He was not tempted by God but by the devil. God allowed it for testing purposes. God meant it for good, but the devil meant it for bad. Jesus was tested, and He passed the tests. He was qualified to do the work. In Genesis 22, God tested

Abraham's faith to see if he would obey Him. The Bible shows us that God allowed people to be tested. The righteous ones were overcomers. Exodus 20:20 says, "And Moses said unto the people; 'Fear not: for God is come to prove (test) you, and that His fear may be before your faces, that ye sin not.'"

I have seen people go through different kinds of tests. I have seen some who seem to be really good people struggling and not having much, but they work hard every day, pray, go to church, and spend time with their families. Then, one day, they receive a sum of money, and they change. They start doing things they did not do before, things that are out of the will of God. They obeyed God when they did not have much, but they could not handle the money. This would have never manifested if they had never been given the opportunity to prove themselves. We who worship God must worship Him in spirit and in truth. God knows but allows the testing so people can see what is in their hearts.

Have you ever seen a person get promoted on the job and then start treating others harshly? You can't fool God. Whatever is in you will come out during testing.

In these two examples, the reverse can also occur. People can go from having a whole lot of money to having none, or they could get fired and have to take any job they can get. Will they steal? Will they become angry and hateful? How they handle it will show them what is in them. God already knows.

In a relationship, what happens when an opportunity presents itself and no one will know if you take it? Do you entertain it, or do you flee? These tests and trials come to let us know what is in our hearts. They allow God to mold us into who we need to be. He is the potter, and we are the clay. In Acts 5:3–5, Ananias thought he was lying to Peter, but verse 3 says he lied to the Holy Spirit, and verse 5 says he lied to God.

God uses people to carry out His work on the earth. The Holy Spirit, which is God's Spirit, can live on the inside of the ones who accept Jesus as their Lord and Savior and obey.

God gave humankind dominion on earth. God will not do anything on earth without a person allowing Him to use his or her body. The Holy Spirit gives the believer the power to do the work (Acts 1:8).

The Holy Spirit will help you understand the scriptures. When we read the Bible, we should ask the Holy Spirit to help us understand, just as the disciples asked Jesus when they wanted to understand the parables He was telling them about the kingdom.

The Holy Spirit is our comforter. He gives us encouragement and strength to make it through our trial and tribulations. When we don't know what to pray for, the Holy Spirit intercedes on our behalf.

We should receive the Holy Spirit and allow Him to help us get to the place God has called us to. We represent Him. We do the things that please God. We are part of His kingdom, and He takes good care of us. The kingdom of God fights for us, just like armies fight for the people in their countries. God's army does not lose. We are victorious.

Ephesians 4:30 says, "Do not grieve the Holy Spirit of God, by whom you were sealed for the day of redemption." For example, some people have said, "That hurt my feelings." Something that they could not see was hurt. Feelings are unseen until they are expressed. We don't want to do anything to offend the Holy Spirit. Just because we can't see Him does not mean we should grieve Him.

As you continue to allow the Holy Spirit to guide you, you will become closer and closer to God's will for your life. You will see the kingdom of God becoming evident in your life daily.

Acts 1:5 says, "For John truly baptized with water; but ye shall be baptized with the Holy Ghost not many days hence." Receive the Holy Spirit. Listen to Him and be led by the Holy Spirit. The Holy Spirit was sent to earth to be with us to help us.

John 16:13 says, "Howbeit when He, the Spirit of truth (Holy Ghost) is come, He will guide you into all truth: for He shall not speak of Himself; but whatsoever He shall hear, that shall He speak: and He will shew you things to come" (parentheses added).

He will not forsake us (Deuteronomy 31:6). He is ready to help us if we will let Him. Open up, receive the Holy Spirit, and allow Him to help you. Do not blaspheme or say anything against the Holy Spirit because it will not be forgiven. If you deny the Holy Spirit access into your life, you have no hope. You will not have a fighting chance against the devil. The Holy Spirit was with Jesus when He went into the wilderness. It is going to take the power of God to defeat the enemy. If you talk against the Holy Ghost, you will not allow Him access and you will have no power to defeat the enemy.

Believe and accept Jesus. Do what the Word of God says so you can be sealed with the Holy Spirit, reunited with God, and back in position. Be blessed in the name of the Father, the Son, and the Holy Spirit.

What touched your spirit while reading
chapter 6, "The Holy Spirit"?

RHONDA VARNADO

CONCLUSION

In conclusion, don't miss the message Jesus wants you to know, the kingdom of God. Begin to seek first the kingdom of God and His righteousness. Trust God. Be sure to fast and stay with the Word of God. Don't focus only on yourself but see the bigger picture. Pray the will of God. There are no shortcuts. Stay within the rules. Jesus is the door. Seek if you truly desire to know about the kingdom of God. Receive the Holy Spirit, and allow Him to guide you.

Printed in the United States
by Baker & Taylor Publisher Services